HERMAN® TREASURY®

Other Popular Herman Books

The 1st Treasury of Herman
The Second Herman Treasury
Herman, The Third Treasury
Herman: The Fourth Treasury
"Herman, Dinner's Served ... as Soon
   as the Smoke Clears!"
Herman, You Were a Much Stronger
   Man on Our First Honeymoon
The Latest Herman

HERMAN ®
TREASURY
5

by
Jim
Unger

Andrews, McMeel & Parker
A Universal Press Syndicate Affiliate
Kansas City • New York

Herman® is syndicated internationally by Universal Press Syndicate.

Herman Treasury 5 copyright © 1986 by Universal Press Syndicate. All rights reserved. Printed in the United States of America. No part of this book may be used or reproduced in any manner whatsoever without written permission except in the case of reprints in the context of reviews. For information write Andrews, McMeel & Parker, 4900 Main Street, Kansas City, Missouri 64112.

ISBN: 0-8362-2083-8
Library of Congress Catalog Card Number: 86-71321

"We shot the decoy!"

"Just a little exploratory surgery."

"Of course I love you, Alistair. I want to have your great-grandchildren."

"Kiss him good night. He starts his new job tomorrow."

"Excuse me. I wonder if you would give me a little push?"

"All I said was, 'I doubt if they'll ever let him sing in the church choir.'"

"I believe patriotism is a good thing here, but not for people in foreign countries."

"I don't know how you can stand to eat those things."

"I was really hoping to be reincarnated as a German shepherd."

"How am I supposed to guess the size over the phone?"

"You wouldn't believe the time I had getting this cake out of the oven!"

"I'd like to see him borrow *this* again!"

"Just because we're outnumbered 100 to one is no excuse for that kind of language!"

"We had to put a steel plate in your leg."

"I've been going to those adult education classes."

"I can't stop."

"If you buy the bike, I'll throw in the parking meter."

"He was very romantic when we first got married, but you know how they change."

"There's no sense spending all our honeymoon money before we get there."

"Dad, we nearly caught a fish *this* big!"

"Let's see ... one cup of coffee and one, two, three packets of sugar."

"If you're the sort of man who can handle a personal income of $500,000 a year, you're the sort of man who can sell our product."

"They've cut the water off, and I need some to cook the potatoes ..."

"Does Dad know about this?"

"He's in the used car business."

"So much for your theory
that the earth is round."

"He's a bit nervous."

"It's me. I think I'm having a nightmare.
Check and see if I'm in bed."

"This'll take about 20 minutes."

"I still think these old statues are more comfortable than the modern stuff."

"If you want to be a grandfather, you've got to make a few sacrifices."

"She hid all my clothes so I couldn't go out tonight."

"What do you want on your hamburger?"

"The wife used to do quite
a bit of modeling ... until
she lost her tube of glue."

"OK. You can put your clothes back on."

"Your mother's been at my wine again."

"Salesman of the week gets to go to Hawaii."

"I never thought I'd see the day when I'd be out of work."

"Get your shoes off. I've just put down clean newspaper."

"He was only 35 years old when he did that one."

"Do you have any special plans for this pork chop?"

"I feel a lot better since I ran out of those pills you gave me."

"Have you got another menu? I can't afford anything on this one."

"Your previous employer says you're unpredictable."

"You wouldn't believe the time we had getting him down those stairs."

"If it looks like a close finish, jump off."

"Same to you!"

"I'm sure you've all been anxious to meet our new company chairman."

"Run out the back and stick 'Happy Birthday' on that for me."

"He'll be 42 years old next month."

"I'm sorry, sir, I just can't find it."

"Got any books about this wide?"

"Cheese omelet, sunny-side up."

"OK, five more minutes, then we'll go somewhere else."

"You'd better cancel the
rest of my appointments."

"Catch of the day is the egg
salad sandwich for $6."

"Chest, 68."

"Is there a band in front of me?"

"Couldn't you hear me knocking?"

**"We didn't reserve a table.
I brought my own."**

**"These all suddenly disappeared
about two million years ago."**

25

"Oh, no! The ink's coming off this twenty."

"I'll have a cheeseburger with everything on it except cheese."

"I just got a late score. Romans 2,168; Carthaginians 1,804."

"And don't let me find out
you're having a good time."

"You name it. I'm collecting for it."

"Two bedrooms."

"Did you see which way
the camel went?"

"OK, here are your exam results."

"I can't listen to you *and* him at the same time."

"You can go back, Johnson, we got the door open."

"He's been driving me nuts since he did that dog food commercial."

"Anybody else like a cake?"

"I thought it was just one
dog in the pet store."

"These clubs are going back to
the store. They're useless."

"We've got 72 pictures of our wedding,
and he's not in one of them."

"Quick. Untie me, Maurice. Your mother's got my credit cards."

"That, my friend, is a Tasmanian dive-bomber."

"OK. I'll be back to pick you up in 25 years. What time?"

"The guy next door has gone away for the weekend. D'you wanna hear a singing telegram?"

"Where's the top of my hot dog?"

"Let's go over to that new restaurant
with the outside terrace and
get some french fries."

"I told you not to open it."

"Is your daughter still
in the same room?"

"This your idea, was it?"

"And you say your bike was chained to it."

"That's perfect, Wayne."

"Don't try to sneak by, sir."

"If you've stopped serving breakfast. I'll have a bowl of corn flakes for lunch."

"I bought you that tie 40 years ago, and this is the first time you've worn it."

"That too close?"

"Will you quit looking at your watch!"

"Rub this on everything within 50 feet of your house."

"We have two sorts of pies: undercooked and overcooked."

"I got a job as a night watchman in a mattress factory."

"You won't be able to write a check with your hands shaking like that."

"Fifteen years in the rat race, Ralph. Who needs it?"

"Don't tell me. Let me guess."

"Is your knee still bothering you?"

"Is the police cruiser still behind us?"

"I am *not* getting angry. I just want to know what you mean by 'triplets.'"

"What do you mean, 'Put up the tent'? That's it!"

"Where did you learn a word like that?"

"There are some gentlemen here to fix the copy machine."

"One day, kid, this will all be yours."

"You're not using enough gunpowder, Harry."

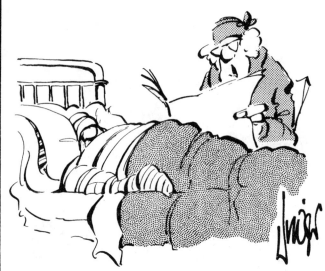

"Your horoscope says, 'Luck is on your side today. Don't be afraid to take risks.'"

"It's quite a friendly neighborhood."

"I'm out of horses until next Thursday."

"Send in the next three patients."

"Is your mommy or daddy home?"

"I told you not to call me
at work after 9 o'clock."

"This is a good one! The guy's trying
to make a date with the operator."

"I wanna try something. Grab
both my legs and push."

"Sorry, pal. I just bought the planet. I want you and all your buddies off by next Friday."

"You must be the new sheriff."

"Where have you been all day? There's a mouse in the bedroom."

"Take a tip, pal. *Never* let them know you can read."

"It doesn't pay to advertise. Someone stole the dog."

"Does car insurance cover ornamental fountains?"

"It's really stuck. Do you think you'll be able to play it like that?"

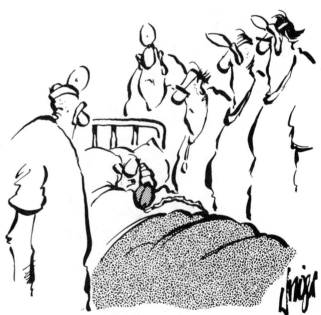

"They're keeping me in for observation."

45

"It's still wobbling."

"Now, now. ... What's all this I hear about you not wanting to come into my nice hospital?"

"Do something, Dad! A big kid at school kicked me in the leg."

"What are you crying for? I promise
you'll have it back by tomorrow."

"I'm giving the goldfish a good swim."

"We'll have to eat in the kitchen.
Your dinner's stuck to the stove."

"The baby-sitter fell asleep and
some gangsters broke in and ate
the rest of that chocolate cake."

"Today's topic is 'public awareness.'"

"Do you realize it's been 12 years since we went through the express checkout?"

"Do you *always* have to buy the cheapest cuts of meat?"

48

"OK. OK. *Not* guilty."

"What can I tell you?"

"It's our anniversary. What have you got that leaves a bad taste in the mouth?"

"OK, don't go crazy every time someone rings the front doorbell."

"You know you're on a diet.
Why do you torture yourself?"

"Just how do you expect me to cook
with these cheap saucepans?"

"Have you ever heard of the book
How to Be Six Inches Taller?"

"Do you mind slowing down?"

"What happened to the picture?"

"I just cut hair. I don't book appointments."

"Our first vice president."

"My guess is that it's doubled back on us."

"We ran out of poached salmon, so I gave you double potatoes."

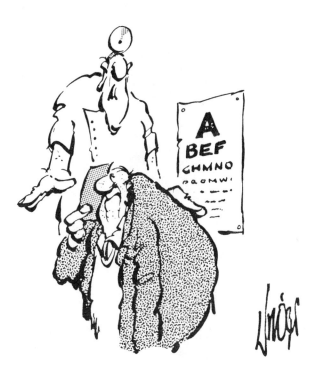

"OK! Now stay exactly like that and I'll move the chart over to the other wall."

"Don't start looking for your glasses at 80 mph."

"Being discharged today! I just spent $8 on these flowers."

"I can't sit in that waiting room all day, doctor. I'm in a hurry."

"'Soup of the day' is the same as the 'soup of yesterday' with spaghetti in it."

"There we are. What's 350 pounds divided by two?"

"I put the kids to bed. I don't want them watching stuff like this."

"Is this No. 11?"

"Anyone would think you're the only person in the world who was ever stung on the nose by a bee."

"I lie awake nights wondering how you get a 10-speed bicycle down a chimney."

"Say when."

"You mustn't play with Grandpa's chair."

"Why did I have to be playing cards
with the boys? For $500 a day,
couldn't you be more creative?"

"Same old Christmas. He bought
me a power saw, and I got him
a pair of gold earrings."

"What are my chances of time
off for good behavior?"

"Mommy's not feeling too well,
so I'm putting you in charge
of cooking and cleaning."

"Can we get some service around here?"

"Just a minute, I can't find my keys."

"I gotta figure out a way to
prevent it from falling over on
its side when it stops rolling."

"Head office wants us to
send someone to the Arctic."

"Why are you still wearing that cap? I've thrown it in the garbage three times."

"I get mixed up with Jupiter and Saturn. Why don't you ask at the gas station?"

"Let's face it, madame. Every swimsuit in this store is going to be a bikini for you."

"Five more minutes. Grandpa's been on his feet all day."

"Did you lock that balcony door?"

"I'll explain later. He had
to go to the hospital."

"I guess you heard about
the floods on Mars?"

"You wouldn't believe me
if I told you how many guys
sit on their wife's knitting."

"Randolph, I'm talking to
a real live brontosaurus."

"Excuse me, sir, do you think I could trouble you to pass the salt?"

"If you must know, I don't like soap in my eyes."

"Muriel, he's gone."

"You expect me to tell the truth, the whole truth, and nothing but the truth, and then you ask me a question like that!"

"Are you joking? Six dollars to send *that*?"

"He says there's definitely no intelligent life down here."

"When you read that letter of reference, you'll understand why I left."

"I don't think I've heard of you before and I'm beginning to see why."

"I can't see Flipper or Goldie!"

"You said we could get a bigger car when the triplets were born."

"I'll let you decide, but they said the electricity will be off for at least an hour."

"I think he's gonna smash the TV if we don't let him out."

"We've been married 38 years
and he says to me 'How do
you take your coffee?'"

"It's 3 o'clock in the morning."

"I told you not to go down there."

"She said she wants to look at
some fur coats on Saturday, so
I'm taking her to the zoo."

"I'm going to ask the warden if he'll let you look after Rusty for a couple of weeks."

"My pet snake swallowed a broom handle."

"You've got to be over at the park at 6 o'clock to fight Henry O'Grady's father."

"How do you say, 'We came to your country to find our suitcases'?"

"I'd like to borrow just enough
to get myself out of debt."

"I need a door like this but with
number 37 on it. ... We're moving."

"I'll serve your dinner as
soon as the smoke clears."

"How's your back?"

"I can hear the ocean!"

"Couldn't you hear me shouting out there?"

"The plumber told you not to block that overflow."

"Drop everything, Joyce. I want you to type this memo."

"What's wrong with this door?"

"Do we set our watches back 4,000 years or forward 4,000 years?"

"Come on ... you won't get to be a guard dog just by looking at it."

"All the kids at your school sent you a get-well card."

"Did you see this? Three rooms of furniture for $15!"

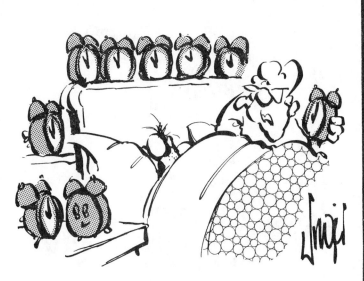

"Only *you* would book a flight at 4:30 in the morning."

"I want you to start jogging three times a week. But not on Woodbine Crescent."

"Are you three all together?"

"I hope you don't expect me to pay for a three-minute lesson."

"Here, kitty, kitty."

"His hospital insurance
runs out in 15 minutes."

"The agency sent me."

"Why don't you write more
clearly? You left a $200 tip."

"If she agrees to cook, I think you could spring for a color TV in the kitchen."

"I hope you realize you let your life insurance run out in 1955."

"Would you like to donate something to the charity of your choice?"

"How can a 2-ounce chocolate bar add on 4 pounds?"

"Your last five dates all went back to their ex-husbands."

"Maurice, he got it home and it was too tight across the shoulders."

"I forgot their crummy password again."

"I doubt if you'd know it. It's a very small country."

"Oh, no! Not him again.
Tell him I'm off sick."

"Table for 650."

"The job's been filled."

"Where did these bathroom
scales come from?"

"He said you put a grape in his ear."

"Is that Robin Hood Pizza?"

"He's been taking trumpet
lessons for two years."

"Twelve years I've been paying
into that medical plan."

"Get down before you hurt yourself."

"The car's not quite as
wide as it used to be."

"I know diamonds are forever. What
have you got for a couple of months?"

"Coffee for me and he'll have a steak
sandwich. ... Separate checks."

"One ... small ... step for worms ..."

"I think you're reeling them in too slow."

"Your previous employer says
you have trouble adjusting."

"Is this your eyewitness?"

"Mother, I thought we'd agreed
. . . 'no luxuries.'"

"They all sound the same
to me after 30 years."

"I don't think you're cut
out for the violin."

"Is it okay if Vanessa
chooses one for herself?"

"Wanna go see a movie, baby?"

"We're demanding more
work and less food."

"The house next door is on
fire. D'you wanna watch?"

"I gotta go. There's a guy
waiting to use the phone."

"You don't have to keep
smiling for a chest X-ray."

"I've lost the keys to my house. Can I live here?"

"Three times I've asked that waitress to bring you a fork."

"The game has been postponed."

"This 'Bottled in 1835' is written in ball-point pen."

"You forgot to tip her."

"I guess you were out back."

"How much to throw this in the ocean?"

"He wants to borrow a million dollars to leave to his grandchildren."

"Okay, three coffees for
him. What do you two want?"

"Golden hits of yesteryear ... 50 cents."

"I told you to get it dry-cleaned."

"He wants to buy an exercise
bicycle with a motor on it."

"My future father-in-law says
you're the best barber in town."

"Got any 25-amp fuses?"

"I have to wear this special shoe
until the swelling goes down."

"Another one of nature's mistakes."

"Harold, I'm phoning you from the car."

"I hope there are plenty of seats."

"I can't find my ticket.
Give me a nice blue one."

"She just polished the floor."

"Why do you always wear
one sock in bed?"

"I've told you a thousand
times to get a new mattress."

"He changed his mind about
paying the electricity bill."

"According to this X-ray,
it's stuck in your leg."

"I'm giving him 15 more minutes
to remember it's my birthday."

"We've been after that one for 15 years."

"As soon as you feel a headache coming on, give your wife two of these."

"I would also like to thank my tropical fish for being there when I needed them."

"Listen ... is that our phone ringing?"

"We used to do quite a lot of ballroom dancing until my arms started getting shorter."

"I'll take over, Wilson."

"D'you want smokers or non-smokers?"

"We ran out of wineglasses. You'll have to sit closer together."

"You can't get a decent
haircut on Saturn."

"I won't be able to eat all of
this. Do you want the cherry?"

"What exactly is a genetic engineer?"

"I taped the cat breathing."

"I hope I'm getting my own room."

"So that's the new MX."

"Oh, no! I didn't read the box.
It's supposed to make 24."

"Yes, Miller, I heard
about your promotion."

"Where did you buy these feather pillows?"

"So much for computer dating."

"He's 50,000 years old. That's three
and a half million to you and me."

"Do you want a game
of dinosaur shoes?"

"I hope all that screaming
is not the one I'm getting."

"He keeps forgetting his name."

"There're only two of these
left in the entire world."

"Can't you give me the speeding ticket
later? I'm really in a big hurry."

"I can't do egg on toast.
It keeps rolling off."

"You need a haircut. It's touching your shoulders."

"Joyce, how much do I charge
people when I don't know
what's wrong with them?"

"Someone gave him a banana
with a file in it."

"Remember me? I sold you
the set of encyclopedias."

"Just put her inside the door."

"Missed it."

"Muriel, I told you this
morning I'd be home late."

"I'll trade the ice cream
for two chunks of apple."

"She didn't want you to kiss her."

"How did you get on at
the weight-loss clinic?"

"I thought so. There's
another peanut in here."

"So I said, 'Bake me a cake
with a hacksaw in it.'"

"I'm having trouble sleeping."

"I'm getting indigestion
just looking at this."

"I've got a pair of aces.
Shall we risk Arizona?"

"I don't know his name! He was
a volunteer from the audience."

"I think he looks much younger
since he dyed his head."

"I got it from a place called 'Greece.'"

"Whatever you do, don't
open your mouth."

"I guess you heard what
happened to me last month."

"Someone's been selling
clarinets to the Indians."

"What's my sponge cake
doing in the bathroom?"

"I took my school report card in
to get it framed and they lost it."

"What's the fish like today?"

113

"I'm gonna count to three. Then I'm going home without you."

"D'you want to look at the menu?"

"What do you mean he'll need a tie to get in? This is my *wife*!"

"Stand back if I catch anything."

"Hurry up. The
tranquilizer's wearing off."

"I don't want to borrow any,
I just want to look at some."

"I don't think I can read any of it.
You're holding it too close."

"I've spent three bucks waiting for you!"

"Is the honeymoon suite
equipped with a kitchen?"

"He took off without paying."

"That dog's driving me nuts!"

"There's one that needs trimming."

"D'you wanna tip me now? Then I'll know what sort of service to give you."

"The little gray bits are non-stick frying pan."

"It's a Siberian mountain dog."

"I just hope you can pay for all these drinks you've been ordering."

"We don't go out much
since he hurt his back."

"If they don't eat leftovers they'll
have to go back to the store."

"What sort of hammer?"

"He never did have a lot of patience."

"The toaster's all clogged up again."

"I know I'm not supposed to interfere, but how's the dog going to climb through that?"

"I didn't want you straining your back plugging in a vacuum cleaner."

"I'd say his chances are about 50/50 of making it to the hospital."

"OK, let's go. But take
it easy on the stairs."

"This should keep you going
while I'm on vacation."

"Commander Zook requesting
permission to come aboard the planet."

"This one's been downgraded."

**"I thought you said,
'Hand over the bunny'!"**

"You been talking to this cactus again?"

"It's our wedding anniversary. She'll have the pasta, and I'll have a roast beef sandwich to go."

"I won't be able to make it next year. I'm having my hair done."

"What's 'The Flight of the Bumblebee' like this evening?"

"You'll have to go back to town. I forgot the mustard."

"Are you nearly finished?"

"I'm not sure what these are, but take them for a couple of weeks and let me know how you feel."

"He can hold his breath for 10 minutes."

"It's a whole different world down there."

"I'll need a full-length photograph
with this loan application."

"Is this your first christening?"

"I can't drink cold soup."

"My old legs are not as
fast as they used to be."

"Banzai!"

"I'm just going to get
a pack of cigarettes."

"They may need a minor adjustment."

"Maybe I should let you drive from now on."

"I'm sorry, sir, you can't come in without a jacket."

"He loves a game of squash."

"The band is not interested in
your domestic problems, Wilson."

"I dropped it in the elevator."

"I hooked a real big one but it
kept swimming around the boat."

"Name?"

"I thought maybe they could identify the person who stole my TV."

"Weren't you supposed to screw them on the *outside*?"

"I lost my watch."

"Hi. Thirty years ago ... camping trip to Arizona ... you lost a little baby boy."

"You're suffering from
very high food pressure."

"This is my oldest son Ronnie's
first wife's sister, Audrey."

"Six years ago he started
putting up a towel rack."

"You forgot the stool!"

"Here he is, Mom. He
fell off the tractor."

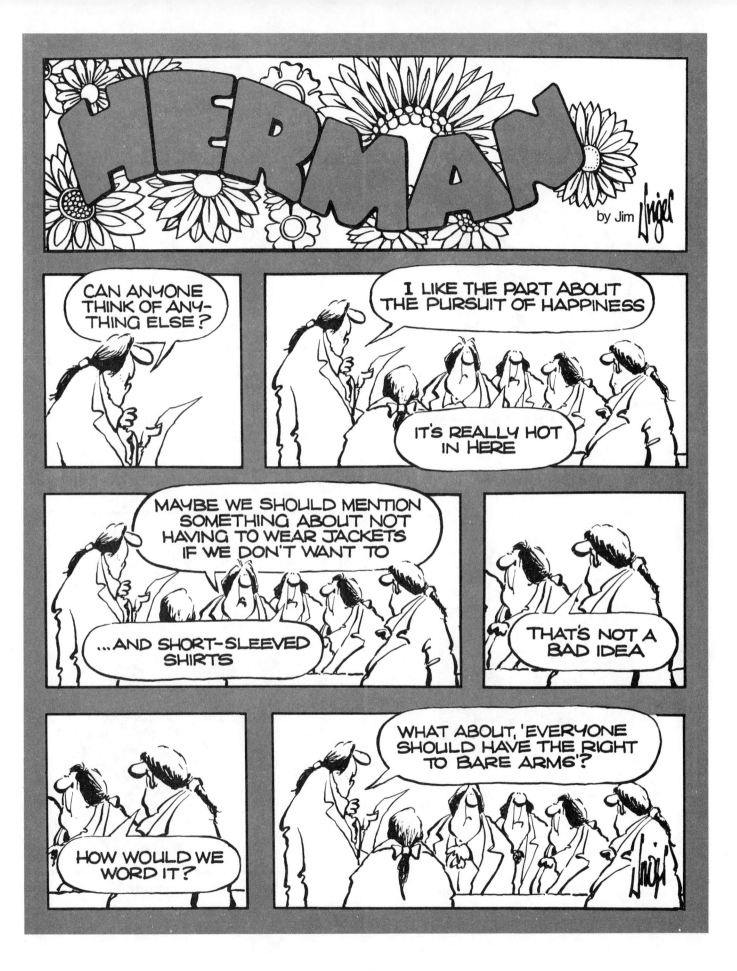

"I'm collecting for Muggers Anonymous."

"How d'you expect me to do all this homework without a computer?"

"I usually do the dishes on her birthday."

"I don't have any money."

"You don't need your teeth. It's soup."

"This is Harold Crudd,
ATV News, Atlantis."

"D'you wanna play blocks for money?"

"Here, your horoscope says, 'Today is
a good day to catch up on all those
little jobs around the house.'"

"Is it OK if I eat while you're smoking?"

"Hang on, grandpa, you'll miss Halley's comet."

"He says the average surface temperature on his planet is about 600 degrees."

"My wife took the car and that came home on its own."

"D'you want me to pull
it off fast or slow?"

"He's working on a way
to make his hair grow."

"We didn't eat all that
junk food when I was a kid."

"Have they removed the saxophone yet?"

"I'd hazard a guess there's
an 'E' on there somewhere."

"I know you got 30 years! But you
still have to pay my legal fees."

"We didn't have any ice, so I put
a piece of frozen pizza in it."

"Do you *have* to remember
my birthday *every* year?"

"All I have available is the honeymoon suite."

"The doctor said you're lucky it wasn't lower."

"I don't usually do passport pictures."

"They won't breed like that! Push the bowls closer together."

"You've got Dutch elm disease."

"Mr. Bixby is out to
lunch at the moment."

"Are they allowed to give me five
parking tickets in one day?"

"I just figured out we can buy
7,800 paper plates for the
price of a dishwasher."

"The dog wants to come in."

"I got a 7-pound frying
pan here last month."

"Dozen long-stemmed roses."

"Can you get that phone? I'm
trying to bathe the dog."

"I've gotta write out a hundred times,
'I must not blow up the school.'"

"To avoid a repetition of yesterday,
I bought you birthday cards
for the next three years."

"Any mail for Number 27, Frank?"

"I've looked everywhere. I
can't find your glasses."

"There's nothing on TV. D'you
want to have an argument?"

"Two cheeseburgers to go."

"If you're thinking of buying lottery tickets, save your money."

"Let's get out of here."

"What do you mean, you 'got custody'?"

"Where else will you get an eight-seater for that price?"

"Do you want to share the cab? I haven't got any money."

"Ralph's poodle wants to talk to you."

"I'm saving for a new dress."

"Kids off school today, Charlie?"

"Not again!"

**"How can I pull it out
without touching it?"**

"Heel."

"I'll have my usual:
two eggs over greasy."

"Three wishes for a dollar."

"I don't think you're strong
enough to get out of bed yet."

"You have been found guilty of forgery."

"Stop me when I get to
something I can borrow."

"I don't think I can take that dripping tap
in the kitchen for the next seven years."

"Have you ever thought about sending
your lunch to an African village?"

"I ran out of newspapers.
Whaddyer want to know?"

"Goodbye and good luck."

"Classic hay fever."

"There must be other jobs
besides being a bodyguard."

"How much is $17 worth in Portugal?"

"Must be the flowers I ordered
for your birthday."

"OK, buddy. Let me see your license."

"I want to exchange these reading glasses for watching television glasses."

"You don't look it."

"I remember this place when it was a volcano."

"So how are you feeling?"

"Give me your name and address.
If I don't end up in the hospital,
I'll send you a tip."

"Have you got $38 worth of quarters?"

"We've only been married six months
and already she wants a new dress."

"You need two numbers
for a pair of hinges."

"He said, 'Glass is a boy's best friend.'"

"Don't believe a word he says, Mother."

"Why should I be the only one to suffer?"

"I've heard of starting things early,
but it's a million years B.C.!"

"I guess that takes care of my Christmas
bonus for the next 25 years."

"These should do it."

"They're still awake."

"Give me a wake-up call around
the middle of next week."

"I don't mind telling you
I'm glad that's over!"

"He's got a sore throat."

"We'll come back later.
She's in one of her moods."

"I'll need a long leash. We live on the ninth floor."

"I like a man who knows where he's going."

"That's the laundry chute."

"I got a job housekeeping for a motorcycle gang."

"I'm second from the left, back row."

"Do you think we'll be on TV?"

"You need more exercise. Go and
get me a cheeseburger with onions."

"Any luck?"

"I was aiming at a hornet."

"So you're the brother-in-law of the
lady who bought the dining room set."

"Don't forget: four doors,
dark blue, power steering."

"... to have and to hold ..."

"I can't eat fast food."

"You said you wanted your eggs over.
Well, they're over the back of the stove."

"I only got halfway there
and it ran out of gas!"

"How do you stop the beans
from sliding into the toaster?"

"Looks are not everything.
She can't cook either."

"We rehearsed all this, Mr. Blunt.
You're supposed to kiss the bride."

"We've got a new chef.
Use lots of ketchup."

"Seen any good movies lately?"

"Didn't you used to be taller?"

"I can't help myself. I'm
gonna spend your gratuity."

"If I don't cure your amnesia
you get double your money back."

"Where do I get stamps?"

"If we can break up the kidney stones, we won't have to operate."

"He's equipped with a spare leg."

"By the time we saved enough for a honeymoon, we didn't want one."

"You've spelled 'eminence' wrong!"

"I used to pay her kid brother to stay in the same room with us!"

"Two hundred and forty-seven submarine sandwiches to go."

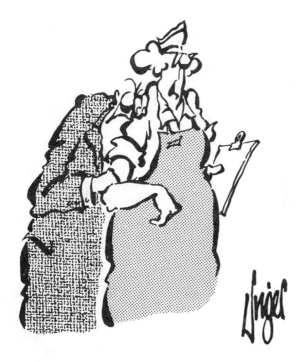

"Doctor, Mr. Mildew is here to see you about his wife's insomnia."

"Sure you've got a choice! The top bunk or the floor."

"She's got that diamond ring stuck on her finger. Got an ax?"

"He's trying to talk!"

"I can't wait to see yours."

"This one looks OK. Can I try it out on your front door?"

"Whatever you do, don't exercise."

"I'm sorry, Harold, but I'm not losing
you on the subway during rush hour."

"I thought you were going
to save me a parking space."

"Let's see ... Niagara Falls ...
Niagara Falls."

"Love your costume."

"I asked him to decorate the kitchen."

"Thirty-nine Primrose Lane, and step on it."

"I've never dated anyone from a circus before."

"Grab your bread roll. It's in my pocket."

"I told you not to order *tuna* in this place."

"That's in case you're in the kitchen."

"If you don't leave me alone, I'll call a mugger."

"Your new next-door neighbor just backed over your china cabinet."

"Your greenflies are all over my bushes again."

"I don't suppose you remember me?"

"Are you the guy who sold me this burglarproof lock?"

"It's the same every spring."

"I'll raise you $200."

"We managed to put the fire out. Just do the front lawn."

"What are frog's legs made of?"

"I won't ask how your day was."

"Call this toll-free number if
you want to cross the street."

"I hope you don't expect me to
make toast with that after you've
dried your feet with it!"

"I couldn't get an extension cord."

"I told your boss you were
going camping for 12 years."

"My foot got stuck in
the cassette player."

"We honeymooned aboard
his 7-foot canoe."

"Sure I've got a charge card!
But I never leave home with it."

"As soon as he's figured out the
steering, he's buying a bike."

"What's the best nail
for hanging a coat on?"

"It's a set of screwdrivers."

"D'you think you could play a little
louder? I keep falling asleep."

"This one just says FOLD."

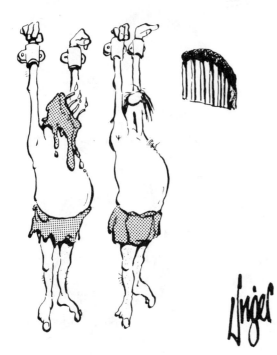

"You shouldn't have told
him it was your birthday."

"It's just a touch of heartburn."

"Eleven and three-quarters."

"This 'Horace the Hamster'
stuff is driving me bananas."

"We will now sing hymn No. 47."

"How many times do I have to tell you to work the other way?"

"They say pets start resembling their people."

"I seem to be losing my touch."

"My wife doesn't like me working late at the office."

"They let us wear our own clothes on weekends."

"He keeps having nightmares about being hit by a ship."

"Here's my bill. That should stop you from smoking and drinking for a few months."

"You're supposed to blow them out!"

"You never give up, do you!"

"He's terrible at making decisions."

"I'll need one other co-signer."

"Dirty-dine."

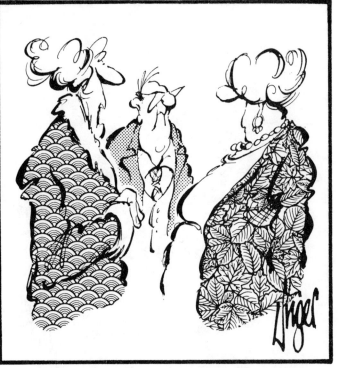

"They took away his library card when they found out he was a bookkeeper."

"Did you say 'grease' or 'cheese'?"

"I told you we should have brought the earth buggy!"

"I really look forward to your visits."

"Maybe you were allergic
to the shellfish."

"You *said* you wanted dinner
served in 10 seconds."

"Will you try to look as if you're enjoying
this ... I'm trying to make a living here."

"Muriel has agreed to marry me again, provided I continue her alimony payments."

"Disgusting! Look at the size of her bathing suit."

"I told him to meet me under the town clock."

"He's been like that for three days after hitting his thumb with a hammer."

"I'm not going through this
every time you go jogging."

"You're not getting enough calcium."

"I don't trust those new-fangled
battery-powered pacemakers."

"Follow the blue line."

**"Watch out, Maurice.
It may be a trap."**

"I see you having a big
fight with your wife."

"You can undress over there, but
watch out for my rubber plant."

"I'll have a glass of water;
preferably 1986."

"My personal computer just told
me to mind my own business!"

"It was a pure accident. He was trying
to cut my credit cards in half."

"I got a date. Mom said I
could borrow your coat."

"Got any clothes with the
initials 'GH' on them?"

"How was I supposed to know you
were in the shower when I flushed?"

"Sir, you're changing
in our display window."

"I know you're cold.
It's cold for all of us."

"What do you mean they want you
to take an early retirement next
Friday without your pension?"

"You may serve the coffee now, Bellows."

"Did you feed this cat?"

"D'you want your change
or shares in the company?"

"Is it OK if he has a chest X-ray?"

"I'm not interested in excuses,
Mildew. You're four minutes late."

"My parents met through a
computer dating service."

"It's coming."

"If you don't like to see me begging in
the street, give me a thousand bucks!"

"Wine production is way up
since we piped in disco music."

"I see you spent 20 years in the Army."

"Listen, I'd better go. That guy's
still waiting to get his clothes."

"She's been here over an hour
and she still can't decide."

"It's a blue 10-speed with
the front wheel missing."

"Can you sign it for me? I didn't bring my glasses."

"Why don't you listen? I said, 'Send over a *can* of glue.'"

"Her previous three marriages didn't work out."

"Dad, I need a note for school tomorrow ... preferably a $10 bill."

"The *other* arm."

"He hates taking a bath."

"We're training to ignore pain and suffering during coffee breaks."

"Harold, you've got to learn to take 'no' for an answer."